Break Through Writer's Block

Invigorate your Mind,
Generate New Ideas, &
Voice your Authentic Message Powerfully

Break Through Writer's Block: Invigorate your Mind,
Generate New Ideas, & Voice your Authentic Message
Powerfully

FIRST EDITION, May 2015

Copyright © 2015 Queen Bee Publisher, Inc.

All rights reserved

ISBN 978-1-62546-010-3 (paperback)

ISBN 978-1-62546-009-7 (digital ebook)

Author: Penelope Gold

Publisher: Queen Bee Publisher Inc., Cheyenne WY

Summary: For writers and non-writers who want to communicate
clearly, this book identifies the 12 main causes of writer's block and
offers dozens of solutions. Students, business pros, and aspiring
authors can finally finish writing their documents.

Topics: Written communication, author, writing documents,
message, overcoming writer's block, novel, essay, report.

Dedication

This book is dedicated to the talented writers in our family:

my daughter Carlynn Katrina
my niece Shelby Erin
my niece Miranda Isabel
my niece Celeste Lunia
and my granddaughter Detriona Jatyii

Keep on writing, Ladies! Continue our family's legacy. You make me so proud.

Contents

1. Introduction 1

    Is This You?.. *1*

    AFTER this Book *2*

  Overview 3

    About the Author *4*

    What Will You Gain from this Book?............................ *5*

2. Get Started Right 7

  Everyday Habits 7

    What's Your Message?..................................... *7*

    Get Inspired *8*

    Vary Your Routine *8*

    Jot Down Notes *9*

    Ask "What If?" *9*

  Your Message 11

    Select a Topic *11*

    Your Authentic Voice *12*

    Let Your Enthusiasm Shine *13*

  Content Prep 15

    Gather Content *15*

    Do Your Research....................................... *16*

    Examples & Stories..................................... *18*

  Writing Tools 20

    Pen & Paper... *20*

    Computer *21*

Word® *22*

Digital Voice Recorder *23*

Voice Recognition Software *24*

Craft Your Document............................27

Location *27*

Writing or NON-Writing? *27*

Speak Your Message *28*

You're In Charge! *29*

Activities..30

3. Solutions for Every Situation......... 31

Causes of Writer's Block *31*

1. Perfectionist 34

Get Comfortable with Messy *34*

Write From Your Heart *35*

Accept Less Than Perfect *35*

2. Analysis Paralysis.................................37

Just Do It *37*

Visualize the Connection............................. *38*

Narrate the Boring *38*

3. Distractions 40

Relocate to a Quiet Place *40*

Get Cooperation....................................... *41*

Self-Discipline *41*

4. Overwhelmed.......................................42

Data Overload – Get Rid of Info.................... *42*

Job Overload *42*

Delegate to Assistant................................. *43*

Partner Up with Friend *43*

Ask Mentor for Help *43*

5. Not Confident 45

    Acknowledge Your Experience Level 45

    Copy a Successful Person 46

    Stay One Step Ahead 46

6. Few Resources 48

    Tool Prep 48

    Topic Pondering 49

    Ask for Help 49

7. Stress 50

    Healthy Routine 50

    Choose a Grateful Attitude 51

    Just Say No 51

    Faith Beats Fear 51

8. Quick Deadline 52

    Get Started NOW 52

    Move the Deadline 52

    Re-Arrange Your Priorities 53

9. Feeling Stuck 54

    Timer – Break - Timer 54

    Start with the Easy Part First 54

    Motivational Messages 55

10. Procrastination 56

    Reverse Self-Sabotage 56

    Begin While You're Excited 57

    Tackle the Tiny 57

11. Stagnant Environment 58

    Vary Your Routine 58

    Soft Background Music 59

    Try Something New & Zany 59

12. Unfocused 60

    Take a Break 60

    Audience of Avatars 62

    Picture Your Goals 62

  Activities 64

4. Super Power Tools........................... 67

  Brainstorm 68

    Start with a Clean Slate 68

    Don't Edit your Thoughts 68

    Creative Ideas into Logical Outline 68

  The 3 Brainstorming Methods 70

    Free Write 70

    Mind Map 72

    Topical Outline 75

  Activities 76

5. Gain Momentum 77

  Become a Better Writer 77

    Read Every Day 77

    Practice Writing 79

    Ask for Feedback 79

    Use Your Resources 79

    Effective Writing 80

  Burger Writing Method 81

    Openings & Closings 82

  Activities 84

6. Keep Going Strong 85

  Bonus Resources 85

Grammar Guide *85*

Vibrant Action Verbs *88*

Transition Phrases & Terms *89*

Hungry for More Courses?... *90*

Book Coaching 91

Bronze Program *91*

Silver Program *91*

Gold Program *92*

Platinum Program... *92*

Activities...94

7. Conclusion..95

Action Steps 95

Summary 96

Contact Me 97

Thank You 97

Bonus Resources...................................99

Grammar Guide...100

Vibrant Verbs..102

Transition Terms...105

Index 108

More Books and Courses.................111

1. Introduction

Do you ever get **writer's block**? That's when you stare at a blank page and your brain is blank, just like the page. I love writing, but sometimes I get writer's block, too. Today, I'm going to share dozens of powerful techniques to break through writer's block so you can finally finish your documents.

This book is for teachers creating lesson plans, instructors preparing curricula, business people delivering speeches, preachers crafting sermons, and project managers writing reports. It's designed for aspiring authors, college students researching essays, and anyone who needs to write anything.

When you complete this book, your mind will be stimulated and you'll imagine new writing ideas. You will learn how to voice your message using your true style to create genuine, powerful documents. Are you ready? Let's get started now.

Is This You?

Is this you? Are you sitting at your desk frustrated, anxious, or unmotivated? Are you drawing a blank when it comes to writing? Do you know what needs to be

said but not how to say it? Or maybe you don't even know what you need to say.

Are you trying to think of ideas but they just aren't forthcoming? Do you have an important project, assignment, or report with a deadline coming up and you don't know where to begin? Or do you just hate writing? If this sounds like you, you're not alone. You're a victim of writer's block. Don't worry, we'll show you how to break through.

Most of us get writer's block at one point or another — even writers. Writer's block happens for many reasons. In this course, we will show you how to break through writer's block and get back on track.

AFTER this Book

After completing this book, ideas will flow through your mind quickly and easily. You will learn how to recharge your brain and generate new ideas — and how to take a break when your mind is stuck. You will be able to start projects, brainstorm, outline, and follow through with your writing.

After you complete this course, you will be energized, excited, and have a new zeal for writing. You will be able to get your story started and be enthusiastic about finishing it. You will start, write, and complete your report or writing project in record time. Let's find out what this book will cover.

Overview

In this book, you will learn how to achieve **5 major milestones**. Then, you will take action steps to accomplish them and get going immediately.

Milestone #1 is **getting started right**. In order to get off on the right foot, you will need to have your tools in front of you, complete your research, and be prepared. Planning ahead helps you un-clutter your mind so that you are focused and ready to write. We will show you what tools you need and share tips on getting started right each time.

Milestone #2 is our **list of solutions** for every situation. In this milestone, you will discover a dozen of the most common reasons for writer's block. I will share techniques for breaking through each of those roadblocks.

Milestone #3 is **super power tools**. I'll share my 3 never-fail strategies for getting all those elusive words, phrases, and ideas onto paper so you can get started grouping and organizing. The tools are free writing, mind mapping, and outlining. I will also show you a demo of cool mind mapping software to elevate your technique.

Milestone #4 is **gain momentum**. I will share excellent evergreen tips that work no matter your topic, style, subject matter, or format. These tried-and-true techniques help you continue the writing process, and become a stronger writer as you practice.

Milestone #5 is **keep going strong**. In this section, I will equip you with tools and resources to continue your development and grow as a writer. I'm pulling out all the stops with my 3 free bonus forms that took me 20 years to compile.

And lastly: your **action steps**. Each section features assignments to complete that will reinforce the training in this course, and get you putting pen to paper.

About the Author

Hello my name is Regina Brown, also known by my pen name Penelope Gold, hence the nickname "GoldenPen". As a professional writing instructor, I will coach you to breaking through writer's block. I'm going to share with you many techniques that I teach in my grammar courses.

I travel around the United States teaching business people how to write better emails, reports, memos, instructions, procedures, and letters. I love teaching grammar, writing, and spelling skills. I authored many published books including my premier book "Buy Your First Home: A Step by Step Guide for First Time Homebuyers". It is published as a printed book, eBook, audio book, and online course.

As an accomplished newspaper article writer, my monthly column is featured in the San Diego Association of Realtors®. I also authored several eBooks that I wrote very quickly — in a day or so. What does that mean for you? You get the opportunity to learn my writing techniques!

I earned my technical writing certificate from California Polytechnic State University, San Luis Obispo. Technical writing is simply taking complex information and putting it into an easy-to-use format so readers can understand and quickly grasp the information. Since then, I have worked at high tech companies writing instructional manuals, online help systems, and policy & procedures manuals. I truly enjoy the technical writing field.

My "how-to" books were written using my technical writing skills; in fact, those skills come in very handy for things like outlines, lists, and bullet points. I'll share some of those techniques with you here in this course.

What Will You Gain from this Book?

Do you have your notebook and pen ready? The best way to begin this course is being ready to learn. What will you get out of this book, "Break Through Writer's Block"? Only what you put into it! I encourage you to take notes, stay engaged, and think of how you can apply each strategy to your specific situation.

You will see hands-on activities at the end of each section. Participating in each activity will get you out of the "stuck" mode and into action.

Lastly, be grateful for the opportunity to learn, grow, and develop your skills. Start each day with an "attitude of gratitude" and you will be blessed beyond measure. A mindset of thankfulness opens you to fresh ideas and forward progress. Let's get started now!

2. Get Started Right

Wouldn't you agree that a little bit of preparation can go a long way toward getting started on the right foot? That's why it's so important to prepare before you sit down to write.

In this section, you will learn the value of getting started right. I will show you how to prepare with techniques, think about your message, and decide how you're going to write. Then, get ready and have your writing tools available. Lastly, we will discuss how to write.

We will start by creating good everyday habits. Find your messages and get inspired by your surroundings. Take notes of things you see as you vary your routine, and most importantly, ask "what if?" Let's get started now.

Everyday Habits

Have you ever needed to write a document, but you didn't know where to begin? Here are a few tips to build your everyday habits that make writing easier.

What's Your Message?

Before you begin writing, **you need a message**. You need something to write about. You need to generate ideas about your topic. Perhaps you've been assigned a topic by your manager and you're having trouble getting started because you're not sure what message you need to communicate. Maybe your goal is to write a book and you don't know where to begin because you're still wondering about your topic. Or perhaps you have an important message you need to communicate and share with others but you don't know the best way to approach the main topic.

We'll cover "messages" thoroughly in the next chapter. Now, let's find out how to get a topic started.

Get Inspired

What's your inspiration? In other words, where can you find ideas? How do you generate your concepts, content, and your main talking points? Often times, we live our lives in a bubble. We get up in the morning, get ready for work, go to work, work hard all day, come home from work, make dinner, feed the family, do homework with the kids, bathe them, put them to bed, and then get ready for work the next day. And this cycle repeats, day after day, week after week, month after month, year after year.

Vary Your Routine

To get inspired, you must **get out of the office**. You need to break out of the daily routine bubble, which can quickly become a rut. Without fresh new ideas, it's difficult to get inspired when your brain gets into a mode of daily habits and routines.

Get out and enjoy an interesting life. Do things you haven't done before. Go to new places. Discover people and situations. Look around at your surroundings. Be curious. Ponder and reflect. Show an interest in people, things, and surroundings.

You're likely to have an idea and an inspiration hit you when you least expect it. That's because your subconscious mind is always working in the background. It is continually processing the activities you do, the things you see, the words you hear, the people you meet, and the situations you encounter.

Jot Down Notes

Your **subconscious mind** is processing those things for you and will invent solutions, create new ideas, and inspire you when least expected. Be ready to jot down notes in a notebook, a napkin, or even a scrap of paper. Always keep your notebook and pen handy.

Write down notes whenever they come to mind; add them to your tickler file. When driving in your car, **keep your voice recorder**, phone, or gadget handy to take notes of your ideas. Once recorded, put these pieces of content in tickler files on your computer.

Tickler files gives you a solid base from which to begin. When it's time to write, just pull content from the appropriate file and begin assembling the document.

Ask "What If?"

Lastly, think about "what if". **"What if"** means using your imagination creatively. The highest paid writers such as Stephen King get paid millions of dollars because they constantly consider "what if".

I always think about "what if?" when I'm writing, whether it's a creative novel, an interesting story, or simply a policies and procedures manual. Procedural manuals are a great way to illustrate "what if" – you're constantly thinking about what's going to happen when the users follow your directions, and what will happen when they don't. What if they choose to push the buttons in a different order than what was recommended in your procedures?

Asking yourself "what if?" as you write is a great way to make sure that you covered all possible scenarios for your topic. When you're working on a group project, a consumer product, or a report to be reviewed by managers, put yourself in their shoes and ask "what if?". Look at all possible scenarios.

You will become a much better writer by frequently asking yourself those 2 little words as you write. It will help you generate new ideas and explore new situations. Thinking about and focusing on the "what if" will rev up your creative juices.

Your Message

As you're writing, perhaps you're not sure what topic you should focus on. That might be the cause of your writer's block.

Select a Topic

As you plan your topic, ask yourself these questions:

- What message do you really and truly want to say to your audience, your readers?

- What message is in your heart?

- Who is your audience, your readers?

- Why would they want to listen to your message?

- What's going on in their lives that you can influence or change for the better?

- How can you convince them there is a better solution that will improve their lives?

- When the readers are done reading, do you want them to take action from your message? What should they do?

- What will be the end result of your message?

- What will happen in your reader's lives after they get your message?

Take a few minutes to ask yourself these questions as you are preparing your topic.

If you believe you aren't an expert at anything, think again. I'll bet you have unique talents, gifts, and skills that you can share with the world.

You have experienced life differently from everyone else, and you learned unique lessons from those life experiences. You can share your experiences, knowledge, and wisdom.

You do NOT have to be the top expert in your industry or your field. You don't have to be the number one known expert, but you do need to be very familiar with your topic and have your own unique, authentic message.

Now, you might be thinking, "Someone else has already written about that topic." You are probably right. In our information era, people can research and find tons of information about any given topic on the internet (often for free).

But no matter your message, you will convey your topic like no one else can. You have your own unique way of viewing or interpreting it. For example, if 10 people went to a conference and they all took notes, they would prepare 10 unique reports — because each person interprets the message his or her own way and communicates it differently. So don't worry if your message is already published. With your unique background, you can discuss any topic from your perspective like no one else can.

Your Authentic Voice

Next is your **authentic voice**. When you're writing, don't try to copy or imitate someone else. Take a moment and think about your topic. Analyze your opinions on it and why you hold those opinions.

What differentiates your perspective from all the other books, documents, stories, articles, and authors that are already accessible? It is your experience, knowledge, viewpoint, ideals, values, advice, trials and successes, and failures. The obstacles you've overcome and lessons learned along life's path frame your distinctive insight. In addition, your background, cultural upbringing, gender, and generation form your unique voice.

So when you write your message, **write from your heart**. Don't just write facts, but give your authentic viewpoint from your heart and let your sincere, true voice shine through. In this way, your message is unique from all others. It doesn't matter how many people have already written about your topic, or how many books have already been published. What matters is your voice, your viewpoint that you bring to the world and how you share with others to give them guidance, direction, and positive encouragement.

These are some ways that you can prepare yourself for writing. And by preparing, thinking in advance, gathering information, and pondering over your topic, you can be prepared when it's time to write. Your words will come quicker. Your ideas will flow and you will be able to craft your message for your audience.

Let Your Enthusiasm Shine

My last tip is to **be excited about your message**. Your message is wonderful, interesting, and exciting. You have the knowledge to change people's lives. Your passion for your topic shows through. Keep that at the forefront of your mind.

Put reminders around you to keep you on track. A visual sample of your book can be stimulated and keep you focused.

When starting a book, I'm excited about the topic. As I'm thinking about my ideas, I use that momentum to create the cover art first. Then I snap a photo of the cover and put it on my screen. Seeing my book cover daily keeps me motivated and on track. It keeps my energy level high, and it gives me the fortitude to persevere through the obstacles that arise.

Content Prep

Now it's time to write
out your notes and turn
your brainstorm ideas
into sentences, develop
those into paragraphs,
and then transform the content into chapters. As
you work, you will watch your document magically
develop right before your eyes.

Gather Content

Next, **gather your content**. Earlier, I talked about
brainstorming things when they come to mind
keeping a tickler file of various topics. Your tickler
file can just be a folder on your computer, or it can
be a paper folder in which you put articles, or both.

Keeping **tickler files** of your various ideas will allow
you to go into the file and pull out content regarding
a particular topic at any given time. I often have 20
or more tickler files with content available at any
given time. It allows me to pull out important
information when I'm ready to write about any
particular topic. I never know when that will be, so
I always have content on hand.

Your **content or resources** can come from **speeches
or talks or presentations** you've given which can be
transcribed easily into typed text. It can be
extracted **from your notes**, from a **meeting** you've
attended, or a **training** in which you participated. It
can consist of content **your diary** or **daily schedule**.

Your content can encompass past **reports, blogs, or
articles** you've written. It may include **interviews**
you've given, or any type of information. I often

write **emails** and think about the valuable content, so I copy and paste the contents to a document for future use. Then, when a similar situation arises, I have the wording handy without having to brainstorm the text all over again.

Become a collector of content. You probably have collected resources on your topic. Look around for old magazines, newspapers, books, courses, training material, notes, or manuals. You may be surprised how much information you already have handy.

Perhaps you have illustrations, graphics, or flowcharts. Search around and pull out any graphics on hand. Did you take photos of this topic? Remember, you can use them for illustrations in your ebook. For example, maybe you started cooking new recipes and eating healthy, and as a result you lost weight and got in shape. I'll bet you can find some before and after photos. You probably also took pictures of the meals you created from your recipes.

Besides content that you've already written yourself, think about **content from other sources**. For example, you probably subscribed to weekly enewsletters in your industry or your career. Also, I receive educational emails from vendors. When I spy a topic or article that's interesting or appealing, I save it in a tickler file to draw from in the future.

Do Your Research

Besides self-generated content and content supplied by others, I also **do my own research**. Sometimes, I don't like to do research until much later in the process. The reason? I don't like to use other people's words, concepts, ideas, or philosophy.

Start by doing some basic research. Many of us begin with the internet. But remember that not every fact on the internet is true. Look for other information that substantiates what you concluded. Caution: don't gather too much information from the internet, as you can easily drown in data overload and will become quickly overwhelmed.

The internet makes it easy to copy others' text. But do NOT copy anyone's information. First of all, copying someone else's work is against the law. That is copyright infringement. Besides the legal aspect, when you copy someone else's words, you are not using your unique voice. Your message needs to be authentic, sincere, and genuine. When I research topics, I analyze messages from various people. Then, I interpret my learnings in my own way, with my own voice, for my own audience.

When I write, I want my content to be fresh and appealing. I use my authentic voice. So I always **start with my own ideas.** Once I've written out everything that I can from my own ideas, I will often do research and find a couple of helpful points from others to also include. The insight from other authors rounds out my document, book, or article with a more holistic viewpoint.

When my document includes references to respected authors, it becomes more comprehensive and credible. Even if sources aren't quoted, including more concepts delves deeper or spans a wide range of ideas on that topic. So gathering content in advance of writing is very important.

Examples & Stories

In your ebook, give examples and stories that tie into your topic. You can gather **examples and stories** in advance. Think of different life situations you have experienced.

Examples help your reader understand your point. It is one thing to state a point, but if you give an illustration or an example of your point in action, people can grasp it, understand it, and visualize it themselves. They're more likely to take action because with a relevant example, they see a clear picture and understand how your topic can affect them personally.

Consider how you can weave a fascinating **story** into each chapter of your book. You know the saying, "Facts tell but stories sell." Everyone loves to listen to a heart-warming story; at the end of your book, that's what people will take away. They will remember how your stories made them feel. Stories, and the emotional feelings, stick with readers much lot longer than facts or data, which are quickly forgotten.

There's a reason why the book "Chicken Soup for the Soul" became an overnight sensation and skyrocketed to the top of the best seller list. The book provides everyday wisdom, morals, and values, dispensed as bite-sized heart-warming stories.

Where can you find stories to tell? You can tell stories that you personally experienced. When you mention other people, I suggest changing their names for their privacy. Perhaps you observed someone else and you can turn that into a third-party story. Again, change the names.

In my books, I often use a semi-fictional story created from several different composite stories. For example, in my real estate book "Buy Your First Home", I tell stories of experiences with home buyers. None of these stories are exact home buyer stories because they are composites of several different buyer experiences. I combined parts of several stories into one experience. I gave fictional names to the characters to protect folks from unwanted publicity, especially if they had to learn a tough life lesson.

Use stories and examples to pull in your readers and get them engaged. Learn to use stories and examples effectively to keep your audience hooked.

Writing Tools

Let's review the **checklist of items** you're going to get ready ahead of time. Here are the items for you to begin assembling:

1. Pen & Paper
2. Laptop Computer
3. Microsoft® Word®
4. Audio Recorder
5. Voice Recognition Software (optional)

Let's discuss in detail these powerful tools to help leverage your time and get more done with less effort. I'm going to share these writing tools with you.

Pen & Paper

My first high tech writing secret is called **pen and paper**. Yep, that's right! A yellow pad with a blue ballpoint pen is my super-secret technique. That is how my best writing starts. I begin with a pen and paper, and as I write with my hand, the ideas miraculously come to mind.

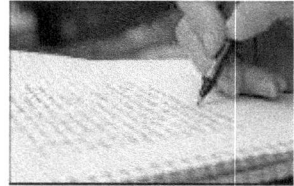

Writing by hand is actually the best method to start writing. When you write in cursive, you activate the creative (right) side of your brain. You will notice that many new, innovative thoughts will appear when writing with the pen and paper.

When you're sitting at your computer typing, it's methodical and process-oriented. It's a logical process that taps into your left brain. The creative side of your brain is not activated and therefore typing does not generate new, fresh ideas.

When writing by hand, it can be difficult to keep up with your brain. Once you start writing, your mind generates more ideas very quickly, and it can be challenging to stay ahead. You have to write very fast so you don't lose the ideas as they appear.

After writing by hand, your content has to be typed out, or "transcribed". Here are a few transcription techniques I recommend:

1. Scan and email your document to your assistant, and have her type it out. She will also correct spelling, ensure sentences are punctuated, add paragraphs marks, insert headers, and organize the material as your arrows indicate.

2. Type it out yourself. This gives you the opportunity to edit as you type. It helps you construct your message clearly, and can minimize your editing at the end.

3. Write handwritten notes on your laptop, notepad, or tablet which has the capability to convert handwritten text to typed text. I use an HP Touch Smart TM2. Read more about computers next.

Computer

When creating an ebook, I prefer a laptop or notebook computer over the desktop version. It allows me to be mobile, yet has the fully functioning advanced features I need. In addition, my laptop offers a really cool feature — I can write on the touch screen! It's perfect for taking notes and scribbling out my ideas when brainstorming.

The **HP Touch Smart TM2** is an excellent notebook computer. It has a touch screen and a neatly-storing stylus. Just open OneNote® software and begin writing with the stylus. After writing your hand written notes, click the "convert" button and your scribbles instantly turn into typed text! Refer to my demo video for a brief preview.

My new **Microsoft® Surface Pro** is also great for writing notes and drawing designs on the screen. This amazing technology is highly accurate. I have found that it recognizes my handwriting and very few corrections are needed. That is why it's one my favorite tech tools.

Word®

You need a computer with **Microsoft® Word®**. If you have an iPad or a tablet, that is okay. However, it probably does not have all the features you need to format and lay out the design, especially if you want are creating a report or printed book.

You will need powerful advanced features to share editing, apply styles, and insert a table of contents. A tablet may be a good way to get started, but probably will not work for your end product once you begin polishing your text.

I found that Google Docs and open software platforms are not fully functional. Therefore, I would advise you to use a laptop or notebook (either PC or Mac) with the full version of Word® — the latest version, if possible. If you are a Mac user, you can select either Word® for Mac or Pages, which also offers full features.

Digital Voice Recorder

Do you give good presentations, but hate writing? That's fine. You can write without writing! When you give your next speech, talk, or instructions, simply connect your digital recorder to the microphone system. Record your words and then they can be typed out WITHOUT writing from scratch!

Before I teach a course lecture or give a presentation in front of a crowd, I often connect my digital voice recorder to the microphone's speaker. My entire speech gets recorded automatically! When done, I quickly and easily send the audio recordings to my assistant. She transcribes my speech and sends it back, typed neatly with punctuation, paragraphs, headings, and lists. I then select the chunks that I want to use for books and online courses. This is a good application of technology.

A **digital voice recorder** is a fabulous tool that helps you get your message out of your mind and into a format that can be shared with others. I call this "writing without writing". An audio recorder will do wonders for helping you get your message from inside your mind onto paper. When you talk your message, you tend to find the right words better and faster than when you are typing.

This cool little tech tool will help you stop procrastinating. Sit down with a rough outline of your document and press the "record" button. Talk about every item on your outline, brainstorming aloud and sharing as much information as you can.

A digital voice recorder is a great way to express your thoughts verbally and then type them out.

Your audio recording will need to be transcribed. Once your thoughts are verbal, there are a few different ways that you can **get them into typed print.**

1. The first method is simply to **listen to it and type it out.** Since we speak faster than we type, use software to slow down the audio. **Express Scribe** is a recommended software. When listening, you can slow down the audio, and pause it on your computer. Remember, as you are transcribing, you also need to add punctuation, paragraph breaks, capital letters, and headings.

2. The second method is to **send your digital recordings to your assistant.** Depending upon how fast you speak, your assistant can transcribe 10 – 15 minutes of audio per hour. Understand that transcription is not instant, so schedule your recordings 1-2 weeks in advance.

I prefer a digital voice recorder over speech-to-text voice recognition software because I like to "talk" my message naturally. I do not like the dictation used some software because you must verbally insert your punctuation. To me, that interrupts the flow as I am brainstorming my message. But, if the software works for you, that's fine. Let's discuss those audio tools now.

Voice Recognition Software

The last tech tool to help you **write without writing** is using **speech-to-text** voice recognition **software.** You speak to the program using a microphone. It listens and it transcribes your audio into typed text.

In theory, it sounds great. Unfortunately, my experience with the computer software, even the expensive paid version, was not satisfactory. There are some downsides to the software.

With your PC or Mac computer, you need to have a **high quality microphone** or wear a **headset**. This can be inconvenient, especially if you are moving around.

Secondly, most software does not recognize sentence structures so you must verbally insert punctuation by saying "period", "comma", or "exclamation mark". That can be really annoying, and may distract you from creating your message.

Thirdly, it doesn't format for you; for example, paragraphs and headings are not inserted. The software does not have the ability to determine your most important points and bold them, or insert bullets points or a numbering sequence, as a personal transcriber would do.

The last downside is that you have to "train" the software. Some versions I tried were highly inaccurate. They were supposed to learn to recognize my words, but it didn't seem to work. It kept getting some of my words wrong, which was irritating and cost me more time than it saved.

Although I chose not to use voice software, you may try them out and see if they work for you. Most computer systems include a free version of voice recognition software. And again, there may be some newer improved versions of the software. See if this is an option for you.

Phone Apps & Tablet

My smart phone has a microphone icon that translates audio intake into typed notes, which is very cool. When I get a great idea, I open my notes app and click the microphone icon to start speaking my message. It absorbs only 2 or 3 sentences at a time, which can be limiting. Your speaking segments must be very brief, but it works in a pinch. For example, when you are traveling and a terrific idea suddenly pops into your mind.

Microphone apps and speech-to-text on mobile devices are nifty, but **may have speaking limitations**. Also, phones are known for running out of battery quickly. That's why I prefer using a digital voice recorder specifically for my writing projects.

These 5 writing tools are great ways to get your words and your message into your document — 2 of them without writing anything!

Craft Your Document

You got inspired, decided on a message, gathered content, and collected your writing tools. Now it's time to begin crafting your document. Here's how to get started with a solid foundation.

Location

You need to find a location that is comfortable yet conducive to creativity. Find a quiet place where you can focus on your message and begin writing. It's important that your "writing hideaway" have **NO DISTRACTIONS** such as phone, email, internet, TV, or other media. That is a reason why so many professional writers go to a "writer's retreat" where they can seclude from everyday life.

Also, make sure that you won't be interrupted by people who want to chat in person. Background noise may be okay, such as a coffee shop or a movie with low volume, IF it doesn't divert you from your task at hand. For more ideas on finding a quiet place, refer to the lecture, "Distractions" which includes solutions for relocating during writing.

Writing or NON-Writing?

If you plan to have your pre-written content available and then assemble it into a document, you will need to plan ahead. Record the audio in advance and type it out before you begin putting your document together.

I call this "writing without writing". It can save you a lot of time and effort. In fact, consider hiring a transcriber to type it out for you. Typing out audio is a simple process task that you can easily outsource. The writing and speaking, however, cannot be delegated, because that's your original voice and your authentic message.

Speak Your Message

Now, you are going to **write, speak, and/or type.** Typing out your content while you write it in your mind is the quickest way to get it done TODAY because it doesn't require any advance preparation.

Get your outline in front of you, and begin writing! **Say everything that you can think of.** As you write, include examples, stories, and the items you researched in advance. Embrace your personality. Let it shine through. Be authentically **you** in your approach.

Don't edit the flow. Follow the order of your outline, but if something else pops into your mind, write it out. You will re-arrange the text later during the polish phase anyway. When you start censoring your words, the creative juices stop flowing. Don't think about spelling or stop to fix typos. Do not edit as you type. Just keep going. If you say something that is not right, do not cross it out. Just write the correct idea and keep going. The important thing is to write as much as you can, as quickly as you can.

If you are a perfectionist (like me), you may get frustrated trying to make your prose perfect in the beginning. Get over it. **Your prose won't be perfect during the writing phase.** A work of art in progress is messy and sloppy. You are going to polish it at the end, so do not try to make it perfect at the beginning.

You're In Charge!

You are your own most powerful and effective weapon. When you think about the value of your message, and make a commitment to yourself, no obstacle can stop you from reaching your goal.

You control your project's success or failure simply by your mindset. Take responsibility, get in charge of your writing project, and get it done! Trust yourself to overcome obstacles and enjoy the taste of victory.

Activities

Here are 3 activities to help you reinforce this section:

1. Name a new location you can go to, or a new activity you can do, that will inspire you and break you out of your rut.

2. Think of a topic and check to see how much content you have already collected.

3. Practice using a digital voice recorder. Verbally speak your book outline and ideas for 15 minutes. Then play it back and listen to your outline.

Start with these simple activities to help you get in the swing of writing and break through writer's block.

3. Solutions for Every Situation

This section is the heart of our course. We show you how to break through writer's block by learning how to overcome a dozen obstacles.

Want solutions to **overcome writer's block?** Here are some of my techniques to break through. They work every time. First, we will examine 12 of the most common causes of writer's block. Then, I will propose several solutions for each of the causes. Of the 38 solutions in this section, surely you can apply a few of them and take action today.

Let's get started now! Get your pen out to take notes of the solutions that you are going to put into action right away.

Causes of Writer's Block

Let's discuss a few **causes of writer's block.** Then I'll show you some effective techniques to get the pen flowing and break through to success. Why do we get writer's block? Let's identify the main causes so that you can eliminate them.

Reasons for your writer's block could be:

1. Stress or anxiousness about a project deadline — or just too many assignments to do!

2. Too few resources. You haven't been given the tools or enough info to construct your document.

3. Being overwhelmed with the topic or overloaded with the thought of beginning a new document. Too much information can be ineffective also; it's difficult to sort through 50 pages of research.

4. A looming deadline conveys a sense of urgency, which may stifle creativity.

5. Procrastination can become a bad habit. Hmmmm... need I say more?

6. Distractions, such as phone, email, text messages, social media, and noise from people talking.

7. Losing focus and concentration when you have to perform tedious work for long periods of time.

8. Analysis paralysis, which is the inability to take action because your brain is over-thinking everything.

9. Lack of confidence in the topic, or perhaps being intimidated by others' expertise on the subject. If you're unfamiliar with the topic, you don't feel like an expert who should be giving advice.

10. Perfectionism can stall your project because you want it to be just right.

11. The "stuck" feeling is a rut that's difficult to break out of.

12. A stagnant environment doesn't foster creativity or new ideas. It freezes your brain.

No matter what the cause of your "brain freeze", let's defrost it now with solutions for every situation.

1. Perfectionist

Are you a perfectionist like me? I always want everything done completely and correctly. I have high standards for those around me as well as for myself. My expectations are through the roof. It's good to have a high standard of excellence, but none of us will ever achieve perfection. Therefore, I have learned to get over myself and my perfectionism because I will not be able to start writing if it has to be perfect.

Perhaps you also are a perfectionist. You delay getting started because you know your document won't be perfect. To overcome writer's block, remember that your document is not going to be pretty. When you start, just accept the fact that the beginning will be messy, but you will polish it at the end. It puts your mind at ease and breaks down writer's block. So in other words, **be willing to free flow and don't filter your message**.

Get Comfortable with Messy

Writing is a messy process. It starts with creating ideas. It involves sloppy writing, scribbles, and disjointed words that don't connect to each other and don't make any sense.

The writing process begins with a scribbled paper full of lines, arrows, cross-outs, additions, and editorial marks. It develops into content groups: ideas marked with various colors or shapes, or out-of-order numbers that do not resemble an outline.

Being a writer means you must be willing to start with the imperfect, then develop and polish until it becomes excellent and nearly perfect.

I remind myself often, "It doesn't have to be perfect. It just has to be done." So if you're a perfectionist like me, repeat that sentence over and over again. This affirmation will motivate you to take action, break through writer's block, and complete your document.

Write From Your Heart

It can be difficult to construct documents based on facts and statistics. It's even harder to write in a vacuum with dry topics, void of feelings. But when you turn on your emotions, and tap into your creative passion for the topic, your writing flows freely. After all, who doesn't enjoy spouting their opinion, thoughts, and beliefs about a topic!

If you have to write a document based on facts or filled with statistics, find a way to inject some personality. Think of the "human element" twist and how the topic affects real people. Write from your heart, drawing on your authentic feelings about the topic. Even if you have to later edit it to tone down the opinions, your writing should be genuine and not generic.

Accept Less Than Perfect

If you hold off taking action until everything is exactly correct and perfect, you will never have a finished document. Be willing to accept the idea that your document will not be perfect when you start. It may not even be perfect when you end.

The most important thing is to take action. Whether you write with your pen, type with your fingers, or talk your message into a voice recorder, do **something**. Make forward progress. Be pro-active.

Perfectionism will hold you back, not only from this book or finished product, but also from future products. You won't be able to move forward and produce more things when you are stuck on the current one.

Remember that phrase and say it aloud, "It doesn't have to be perfect, it just has to be done." And be willing to take **action** and do it **now**.

2. Analysis Paralysis

That's a funny term. What is it, exactly? It's a name for a person who is methodical, logical, and over-thinks everything. A person who has "analysis paralysis" has a difficult time making decisions because they are always looking for more facts to justify their decision before taking action.

Analysis Paralysis is a symptom of people who fail to take action because they are overly analytical. In their mind, they are thinking through solutions: researching data, gathering facts, analyzing and comparing them. While it's good to have information at our disposal, and it's even better to think through our decisions, a person with analysis paralysis can't start writing because they cannot make a decision. They are stalled and can't get started.

Just Do It

The cure for this is to recognize the symptoms of your personality, and get in the habit of taking action. **Action** is the strongest habit to overcome analysis paralysis. Whether that action is writing out your message, jotting notes on a piece of paper, editing it on the computer, or even speaking into a digital voice recorder, you will **gain momentum by taking action**.

You've heard the farmer's saying, "I would rather see a field plowed crooked than a field unplowed." It speaks to the importance of taking action, even if it's not perfect. By doing nothing, you hold up this message from being delivered to your audience.

More importantly, you impede your future messages. You cannot share forthcoming messages when they are backlogged. So if you're stuck because can't decide what to do, the remedy is to take action. Do **SOMETHING!**

Visualize the Connection

Picture your audience and how they will feel when they receive your message. In your mind, picture yourself talking to one of your readers. What would you say in person? How he or she react? What would you tell a group of interested people about this topic?

What if you were speaking to an audience of hundreds of readers? What message would you convey? How would your readers feel? Would your message spur them to action? Would it be useful and effective? What would they do, once they digested your message?

Visualizing a reader, and your connection to that reader, will help you break through writer's block. You'll be able to construct your message to target your reader's needs.

Narrate the Boring

Since you know that you are going to delete the narrative wording and long-winded prose, you want to just skip it and get down to the nitty-gritty, right? Wrong. Sometimes "cutting to the chase" causes writer's block.

Start at the beginning and write down everything you can think of. Write out a long intro, even though you know you will later delete much of it. Go ahead and begin at the very beginning of your story. Write out everything that comes to mind. Tell all the details. That gets your mind engaged and on track for your topic.

Yes, you will have to go back later and edit out the extraneous material that's not relevant to your document. But it's worth the time, because writing out the background helps shift your mind into gear and break through writer's block.

To summarize: **Action is the antidote for analysis paralysis.** Action unlocks your mind and affords you creativity. It gets the ball rolling. When you take action, you gain momentum so you can continue on with your message.

3. Distractions

It's easy to get distracted in our modern society, isn't it? Distractions are when people, media, situations, and gadgets are competing for our time and attention. For example, you're sitting at your desk trying to write. Your phone rings and interrupts you. Next, an email pops up. Then, a co-worker stops in to chat. Or, you visit the internet to answer a research question and get distracted by flashy ads. Perhaps you pick up your mobile phone to make a call, but then glimpse your friends' social media posts, and now you're off track again.

The keys to protecting your quiet, creative space and eliminating distractions are to:

1. Find a quiet place.
2. Get the cooperation of people around you.
3. Set your boundaries using self-discipline.

Relocate to a Quiet Place

To find a quiet place around you means that you may have to relocate. In fact, it's probably better if you don't do your main writing at your desk. You may have to sneak away into somebody else's office and shut the door, or hang a sign on your door, "In A Meeting".

Find a different place where you can focus. By going to a different location, you don't get distracted with the normal ordinary things that disrupt your flow. In a new location, you have a fresh mindset that encourages creativity.

Get Cooperation

The second tip to prevent distractions is to inform those around you. Let your co-workers, friends, business associates, and family members know you're committed to finishing an important project that you are. Ask for their cooperation to allow you uninterrupted quiet time. Give them an incentive by promising a reward at the end.

For example, "When my project is completed, let's all go to dinner together and celebrate." With an incentive, they will be motivated to cooperate and to keep distractions away from you. They now have a vested interest in helping you finish your project.

Self-Discipline

The third way to eliminate distractions is to practice self-discipline. For example, make it a habit to turn off your internet and your email. Prevent social media posts from popping up on your phone. And if they do, turn off your phone. Go to a quiet location where you know you won't be distracted. Stay focused and concentrate. And, of course, make sure that you're not distracting yourself either!

These are the 3 keys to overcoming distractions so that you can focus clearly and begin writing. Break through writer's block by creating new good habits.

4. Overwhelmed

Being overwhelmed means that you just don't know where to begin. You have too much information, data, or research. Yes, it's possible to have too much information. That causes a mental block and can make you want to give up.

Data Overload – Get Rid of Info

One technique for breaking through the overwhelm is to **remove the info from your desk.** For example, you researched a topic on the internet and found 55,000 links. Select 3 and save those to your tickler file. Then, turn off the internet because you don't want to be overwhelmed by the 55,000 other links.

Job Overload

On a human level, maybe you're overwhelmed with your many responsibilities and duties. There are too many tasks on your plate and you don't know when, or if, you can ever accomplish it all. As a professional, partner with people who can be part of your writing team. The 3 types of team members who can assist you are the following:

- **Assistant**: Delegate to an apprentice or assistant
- **Partner**: Share responsibilities with a business partner
- **Mentor**: Lean on the strength of a seasoned, experienced mentor

Delegate to Assistant

This is a good time to **delegate to other people**. Delegate as much as you can, as often as you can. Ask yourself, "Am I the best person to do this task or can somebody else do it?" Even if they don't do the tasks perfectly, it's okay to delegate. And remember, that after they complete the tasks, you must verify the work was completed correctly because ultimately, you are responsible. Keep training your assistant or apprentice until they master the tasks.

Partner Up with Friend

Select somebody to assist you: a team partner with whom you can develop mutual accountability, encourage each other and create a positive synergy. You can't always "see the forest for the trees", as the saying goes. But from an airplane, you have a bird's eye view of the forest and you can see the paths clearly from your overhead perspective. In the same way, a team partner, business associate, or accountability partner can see your direction and point it out. You can brainstorm and bounce ideas off of each other. It's a great way to elevate your innovation.

Ask Mentor for Help

Consider getting a **mentor to guide and direct you.** Seasoned pros have experienced many of the same obstacles you face. They can guide and direct you in the areas you're struggling. Don't re-create the wheel. Just copy others who have already been successful in your industry. Whatever steps they took that were successful, you can do the same thing too, except better. Look for a person who can coach and advise you.

So the **3 ways to overcome job overwhelm** are: **delegate to an assistant or apprentice**, to **have a partner** to share duties and cover for each other, and **get a mentor** to guide you and give direction.

5. Not Confident

Maybe you are not confident
that you know the topic well
enough, or you're intimidated
by others' expertise on the
subject. Perhaps you lack the
confidence of a subject matter expert. You don't
view yourself as an authority on the topic. And if
you doubt yourself, others will doubt you too.
Perhaps you are afraid that your audience may
criticize your lack of knowledge.

You think that others are better equipped than you
or they know more about the topic than you do, so
you hesitate to get started — and that can cause
writer's block.

Acknowledge Your Experience Level

The solution is to acknowledge that you're not the
world's best expert on this topic. Okay, so you don't
have a PhD, you haven't been quoted by Oprah, and
you don't have a book on the New York Times best-
seller list — and that is fine. As long as you know
more than your audience, that is what counts.

For example, if your audience consists of first-time
home buyers, and you have experience with the
home purchase process, you can explain what you
know. You don't have to be the top expert in the
whole world to be able to advise them. You just
need to know more than they do. Stay one step
ahead of your audience. It's okay to let your readers
know that you're at the intermediate level, if the
material is geared to beginner level readers.

Copy a Successful Person

Identify a successful person and walk in their footsteps. Do what she did — except improve it and do it even better! "It's okay to be a copycat as long as you copy the right cat." I love that saying because you use a template, rather than re-creating the wheel.

If someone else has already completed a complicated project, you can do it too. It gives you confidence know that the task CAN be done. Find a simple system that you can follow. Remember not to copy others' text or artistic renderings unless you have their written permission. You don't want to violate copyright laws. The concept is to follow their success system, not to plagiarize their text or materials.

By observing successful people, you will discover their formula and adapt it for yourself. Knowing that you are on the track to success can give you confidence to break through writer's block and help you begin writing.

Stay One Step Ahead

Stay one step ahead by **researching your topic and** ensuring that your document **reflects expert viewpoints.** While writing, don't compare yourself with a competitor. It can intimidate you to view their materials. You may start thinking, "I can never do an amazing job like this person did." And then you have defeated yourself before you even started.

Embrace your passion about the topic. You are enthusiastic and zealous about this subject. And because of that, it has led to curiosity and you have more experience and more information than most people — and that is all you need.

If you have confidence in yourself, others will have confidence in you as well, and they will respect you as an authority figure. Apply the above 3 techniques to build your confidence so you can break through writer's block and get started writing today.

6. Few Resources

The first solution is to **make sure you have all your materials in advance.** When you feel prepared and confident, writer's block evaporates. Do your research ahead of time so you feel confident of the topic.

Tool Prep

Did your manager give you an assignment, but not enough tools or info to complete your project? Did she assume that you already had the tools or that you could figure it out? In that case, maybe you have too few resources to begin writing — and that can cause writer's block.

Start gathering your resources as early as possible. Whether it's a tool you need to write or the actual content itself, have everything easily accessible. Perhaps you need information, data, facts, or statistics. Maybe you need a credible quote from an authority figure or you need illustrations, examples, stories. Do you need to include a graph? If you can't find one, use a chart or photograph that illustrates your point.

Earlier, we discussed the technique of being prepared in advance by gathering content, researching your topic, and jotting down your ideas. Ask yourself what tools you may need. If you don't have them, don't let that hold you back from getting started. Get started anyway and then make a list of what you need as you go along.

Topic Pondering

Often, I begin my writing by thinking about my topic well in advance. Before I even scribble a note on my notepad, I ponder it and mull over the topic. I let the ideas percolate through my mind for a few days in a row. I allow my subconscious brain to gather ideas and start assembling a mental outline.

Thinking it through it in advance helps me realize what resources I will need ahead of time. The bottom line is: begin thinking about your topic in advance. Let your subconscious come up with ideas. And if you don't have enough resources, don't let that stop you from getting started.

Ask for Help

To find out what resources you need, I recommend talking to someone who has already completed a similar task or project. Find out what tools they utilized to be successful.

Lastly, it's okay to go back to the person who expected you to complete this writing assignment and ask what tools are needed. Once you begin writing or creating your document and putting it together, you will discover what it missing and you can assertively ask for more resources. Or, show initiative and search for those tools yourself.

7. Stress

Stress can be physical, mental, emotional, spiritual or relationship driven. It can be work related, personally related, or just the overwhelm of day to day life. Stress is often hidden until it appears in many forms. We are often so busy that our body is operating at a high stress level. While we believe we're being productive, a high operating level can be actually counter-productive. When you pause and try to write, those hidden stresses rise to the surface. They can block your mind and inhibit writing.

Healthy Routine

Break through writer's block stress by having a **regular, healthy routine of eating, sleeping, and exercising.** When you have not had enough sleep, you get tired and cranky, and you don't even realize it. Exercise stimulates your brain and your mind. Good nutrition fuels your mind and energizes your body. Sleep (and rest) helps you function at a peak level.

Eliminate stress by leading a healthier lifestyle. Make it a habit to have a regular routine of going to bed early, getting plenty of sleep, exercising every day, and eating healthy nutritious meals at regular times every day. If you can add these healthy habits into your daily routine, you will see stress diminish.

Choose a Grateful Attitude

When stress, doubt, or fear creep into your mind, push them back with your thankfulness and appreciation. Now is the time to cultivate an attitude of gratitude. Think about all the many blessings in your life! Your stress will begin to fade as you replace it with happy thoughts.

Just Say No

When we keep putting more projects on our plate, after a while the overload causes stress. Often, in our desire to achieve and accomplish, we take on much more than we should. The desire to please everyone can be a self-sabotaging behavior. **Develop the ability to say "no"** to taking on new projects. Learn how to say it politely yet assertively. For example, "In order for me to start a new task, I would have to stop a current task. How do you want me to prioritize the tasks you've assigned to me?"

Faith Beats Fear

If fear is causing stress in your life, you can combat fear with your faith. You've heard the saying, "I'm too blessed to be stressed."

One of my favorite books is *"30 Days to Taming Your Stress"* by Deborah Smith Pegues. It's an awesome little pocket book featuring 30 different techniques for eliminating stress in your life each day. I love the author's philosophy about causes of stress including conflicts, past hurts, and high expectations. She offers wonderful, calming, bite-sized activities that we can implement to de-stress ourselves every day.

8. Quick Deadline

You have a tight deadline and that is causing writer's block? It is ironic that knowing we HAVE to write quickly makes our brains freeze up and we can't spit out any words. If you have a tight deadline, consider these solutions.

Get Started NOW

The key to fulfilling a quick deadline is to **get started right away!** Do as much as you can, as quickly as you can. However, be assertive and let your manager know that you will commit to a realistic production level. You will be responsible for accomplishing as much as humanly possible within the time frame allotted.

Move the Deadline

First of all, **don't take on projects with such tight deadlines**. You've heard the saying, "Your lack of preparation does not constitute an emergency on my part." In other words, when someone has not adequately planned ahead and he or she asks you to meet their tight deadline, request to move the deadline to suit your schedule.

Be assertive and let your manager know that you cannot finish in such a tight timeframe, and request additional time. Perhaps, you are a business owner or an independent contractor. If so, consider turning down last-minute "rush" jobs or charging an additional fee (because you would have to halt other projects).

A tight deadline can pressure you to produce high quality material in an impossible time frame. I suggest that you **review your deadline** and see what you **CAN** accomplish within the time frame required. For example, maybe you won't have the entire book completed within 2 weeks but you can have a rough draft ready for review. So instead of thinking of what you cannot do, **think of what you can do within the time frame** that gives you a more accurate idea of how much you can accomplish and when.

Re-Arrange Your Priorities

Change your priorities to focus on that task with the quickest deadline. You'll have to re-arrange the order of your tasks and put less critical projects on the back burner. With a tight deadline, accept the fact that other tasks will fall by the wayside. Be comfortable with putting other projects on the back burner temporarily. Don't try to do everything and be everything to everyone.

Be careful not to compromise the healthy life habits that you developed such as adequate rest, proper nutrition, and daily exercise routine. When you start to compromise your health, you may feel overwhelmed or become ill. You can't churn out quality projects unless you have optimal health.

9. Feeling Stuck

Are you feeling stuck? You don't know where to start and you don't know how to start. To get unstuck, we reveal 3 solutions for you below.

Timer – Break - Timer

Try this method: **set a timer** and write non-stop for 10 minutes. Take a 1 minute break, then write for another 10 minutes. Repeat that pattern 5 times or until you are done.

You'll be surprised how productive your mind becomes. During the time you are taking a conscious break, your subconscious is still working hard to generate ideas.

Start with the Easy Part First

Maybe you're procrastinating because you need **momentum**. The answer is to **start with the easiest topic or subject**. Begin with the section you know best, and write it first. Once you write out the easiest area then do the second easiest, and the third easiest. Sometimes I start at the end, in the middle, or even skip around. It doesn't matter what order it gets written, as long as it all gets done.

Instead of writing in a logical sequence of chapters, begin writing the easiest parts first. By the time you get to the difficult areas, you will be nearly finished. The difficult areas will then be conquerable because you can see the progress. Leverage the power of momentum and use it to your benefit.

Motivational Messages

My favorite audio seminars are from workshops I attended, such as *"Success Self-Programming"* by Lee Milteer and *"Getting Unstuck"* by Dr. Sidney B. Simon. Every time I listen to them, I feel energized and inspired to take action. Try listening to an audio CD or mp3 with a motivational message.

Over the years, I have collected dozens of audio workshops and lectures and learning messages. I listen while I'm driving in the car, and sometimes when working in my office on Saturday mornings. Encouraging messages can help you take action and create positive energy.

10. Procrastination

Procrastination is one of those human nature principles — putting off things that we don't like to do until the last minute, and the tight deadline then causes stress. **Procrastination is a form of self sabotage.** It means that we indulge ourselves by doing things we love to do first, ignoring tasks we hate doing until the last minute.

Procrastination is not a good technique it puts pressure on you and affects those around you. Unfinished tasks leave a dark cloud hanging over your head and you really can't move forward with your life until you finish those undone projects. It locks up your mind and creates a silent burden.

Reverse Self-Sabotage

The key to overcoming procrastination is to realize that it's a form of self sabotage. Ask yourself why you are doing this to yourself. Is it because you really don't deserve something good? Or is it because you thrive on the adrenaline of waiting until the last minute?

Perhaps there is a hidden agenda. For example, you really detest this topic because of a previous experience. Perhaps you're being forced to write and you procrastinate to rebel against your manager. Understanding your reasons for procrastinating will help you get a handle on it. You want to change your behavior and develop better habits for yourself that are more productive, positive, and successful.

Begin While You're Excited

To overcome procrastination, **get started right away**. When you first get assigned a topic, you're enthusiastic about it. Immediately, write down everything you can think of about it. It gets you started on a positive foot and you don't dread working on it. When it's time to complete the project, it's easy to do. Simply continue the momentum you've already started.

Tackle the Tiny

Another way that I overcome procrastination is by doing something little, small, and insignificant at first. Once those small things are tackled, then I have the confidence to tackle the larger things.

If you do all the little things that are easy to complete and you find that you're 70% done, then it's very easy to tackle the 30% that you thought was hard. Your document is almost done and it's a lot easier to finish the last few items.

You've heard the saying "How do you eat an elephant? One bite at a time." And that's how you finish big assignments — just accomplish one little thing at a time every day on a consistent basis. Soon you will have completed it all without even realizing that you have finished.

11. Stagnant Environment

Do you live in a bubble? You get up, go to work, and then come back home and get ready for work the next day. Has your life turned into the proverbial hamster in the wheel, running a hundred miles per hour but never getting anywhere? It creates a **stagnant environment that blocks writing creativity**.

So many of us live in a bubble. We have difficulty thinking of new ideas because we are in a rut with our daily routine. We go to our job, work all day, and then go home. We make dinner, help the kids with homework, and put them to bed. Then we get ready for the next day and start all over again.

Vary Your Routine

To generate fresh, creative ideas, you need to **break out of your rut**. That's another great reason to write your document in a new environment or different location, rather than your home or your office. It helps your mind to think creatively and break out of that bubble.

While sitting your desk, emails pop up and your phone rings. People stop in to chat. You have to prepare reports, process tasks, and rush off to meetings. By going to a different geographic area, your mind turns "off" the work mode and turns "on" the creative mode. Borrow someone else's office, or sit on a bench outside, or "hide out" at a quiet coffee shop. That's just what the doctor ordered to help you generate new ideas for writing your document!

Soft Background Music

Turn on light jazz, gospel, or classical music softly in the background. It should be upbeat and inspirational, yet quiet and non-intrusive. It can ramp up your creativity subconsciously.

Soft music should set the tone for productivity without distracting you from thinking. I prefer continuous music without words, and definitely not radio stations with ads. If you find yourself focusing on the music, turn it down or change the channel.

Try Something New & Zany

Break out of your comfort zone by doing a new, fun, and exciting activity. Even if you only try it once, experiencing a new activity can open your mind to possibilities. Here are a few ideas:

- Take a one-day seminar. You'll meet new people, brush up on a topic, and enjoy a fresh location for the day. I bet you will get some great ideas too.

- Plant a garden in your back yard. Gardening is a good activity that allows your mind to percolate.

- Ride your bicycle into town and back. When I ride my bike, it's a nice quiet route and God talks to me during our "alone" time.

When was the last time you went to the zoo alone, without kids? How long has it been since you took a boat ride or toured a museum? What about something wacky and zany, like riding a roller coaster or playing in the snow?

12. Unfocused

Our last reason for writer's block is being unfocused. The lack of focus can actually be caused by concentrating too much.

Is your mind starting to wander? You've been working on your writing project for a while now. And you can no longer focus. You ran into writer's block. One of the major ways to overcome it, ironically, is NOT to focus more — but rather to take a break.

Take a Break

When you find it difficult concentrate, **take a break**. In the middle of focusing and concentrating, sometimes you can accomplish more by pausing and giving your brain a brief break. When you take a break, your conscious mind pauses because you told it to stop work. Your subconscious mind, though, is still moving rapidly, generating ideas for you in the background.

Let's look at 3 different types of breaks you can take: micro break, stretch break, or walking break.

Micro Break

When you get a mind stalemate, take a **"micro break"** and switch up the project you're working on, or simply turn to a new part of the project. You don't need to get out of your chair. Just switch your focus to a different part of the project. Instead of working on the first chapter, turn to the end and start on the last chapter. Rather than editing paragraphs from start to finish, begin at the end and edit going backwards. I bet you'll be surprised at the results.

For example, you are at an impasse on Chapter 3 so you jump ahead to Chapter 5. But while working on Chapter 5, all of sudden, a great idea for Chapter 3 pops into your mind. You are going to have to flip back to chapter 3. And that's okay! You don't have to write in order. Write it in any manner it comes to mind. You can always go back and organize the content later. The important thing is to get the content out of your mind and onto paper.

Stretch Break

The second type is a **"stretch break"**. That's when you actually get up from your desk for a minute and walk across the room, or stretch. By doing this small, simple activity, you give your brain a chance to generate a new idea. That's a great reason why I advise placing your printer across the room. When you print out something, you have to get up and go get it, and it gives your mind a quick break. Try taking a healthy break by standing behind your chair and doing a few stretching exercises.

Walking Break

A **"walking break"** is when my brain just cannot function anymore because I am on overload or my legs start to get restless from sitting so long. I feel like I need to get up and move around. For 5 or 10 minutes, I walk outside to get a breath of fresh air, down the street, or maybe even around the block at a very quick pace.

After taking a break, you'll be surprised at the new ideas you come up with because your subconscious is still generating ideas in the background. When you get back to your desk, your mind will be sharp and you'll feel like you have a fresh start.

Audience of Avatars

An avatar is an icon or image that portrays your readers. It's a symbolic figure that represents a typical person who is going to read your document.

If you're a business owner, you probably read the book, "The Inmates are Running the Asylum" by Alan Cooper. The author suggests creating "personas" — sketches of 3 sample customers who can represent your most frequent clients, users, or readers. Name each "avatar" and assign a background history. As you write your document, stop and ask yourself, "How would <Avatar 1> interpret this topic?"

Continue to view your material from their points of view. This makes your audience come alive for you. When drafting your document, you can focus on 3 sample readers (often a composite based on real people you know), and it helps you craft a specific message for your real readers.

Picture Your Goals

Make a dream board that highlights your goals visually, in big vibrant colors. Assemble a large poster board with family photos, and magazine pictures that represent your "why", your life purpose, or the results from this large project you are about to take on. Why do you do what you do?

"A picture is worth a thousand words," speaks to the power of visualization. Before you embark on this large project, take a few moments to consider its long-term benefits for you. What will you gain from this sacrifice of time and effort? A large full-color poster filled with your goals and favorite things can motivate and inspire you to keep going despite challenges, obstacles, and uncertainty. It reminds you of your "why".

Activities

Now that I have shown you 12 reasons for writer's block and given you solutions to overcome each of those, it's time to do some activities that will help you apply these techniques right now to your current situation.

1. Take out a piece of paper and a pen. Write down one cause of your writer's block. What are you going to do to solve it? Write a solution and how you will implement it. By writing this out, you've already taken action and broken through writer's block.

2. Try the "Timer – Break – Timer" solution. Set your timer for 10 minutes and write non-stop. Don't edit or censor as you write. Then take a 1-minute break. Set your timer for another 10 minutes and write again.

3. To relieve overwhelm, who can you rely on to help you? Write down the name of 1 person to whom you can delegate tasks, 1 person with whom you can partner, and 1 person from whom you can ask advice.

4. Create 3 avatars, or personas, of sample readers. Include an illustration, demographics, and a brief history for each person. Ask yourself how each of these 3 sample readers would benefit from your document.

5. Make a dream board to depict your "why". It only takes about 30 minutes, and can last you all year long. Hang it near your desk where it can motivate and inspire you to keep working hard!

To the 12 causes of writer's block, I've shared 38 different solutions! Find a few that work for you and practice frequently. Now, I'm going to reveal my treasure chest of super power tools to help get you started on a big project such as a book, year-end report, or procedures manual.

4. Super Power Tools

Another cause of writer's block is **sitting at your computer, staring at a blank screen.** Your computer is a machine and your keyboard is a process-driven tool. Creativity cannot thrive with the tedious typing process.

Grab a pad of paper and a ballpoint pen, and **write with your hand.** One of the best techniques for overcoming writer's block is to use a pen and paper because your mind taps into the creative side when your hand starts writing. You will find that your creative juices will start to flow. The more you write, the more ideas you get — in fact, you will probably get ideas faster than you can write them down.

Here are my brainstorming strategies that are great strategies to banish writer's block:

1. Free write
2. Mind mapping
3. Outline

I will show you how to brainstorm using these 3 great techniques, including a mindmapping demo. Then you will break through writer's block and write your document. Let's get started now!

Brainstorm

The first step in producing your document is brainstorming. It all begins with thoughts, words, and ideas. This is the heart of your message.

Start with a Clean Slate

Instead of thinking about what other authors have written, or what you have read before, empty those thoughts from your mind. Begin with a blank page and NO pre-conceived ideas of your topic. **Start with a clean slate.**

Forget about what other experts say and other's opinions. Instead, focus solely on your message. Do not worry about other books and other research.

Think about what you envision for **your reader**. Worry only about your own message. Start with your fresh idea. Be authentic, sincere, and original. Write from your heart.

Don't Edit your Thoughts

Keep going strong! Do not stop and think about spelling or grammar or punctuation. When you censor your brainstorming, you interrupt the flow of thoughts. Remember, you can always delete things later. It's easier to delete than to add content later. Now is the time to put all the information in your document.

Creative Ideas into Logical Outline

Okay, you have all that rich content on paper. But it looks messy and disorganized. How do you make any sense of it?

The next step is to **group similar items together.** These are closely related thoughts, ideas, and phrases. I like to group content by highlighting similar sentences with colored highlighters or marking them into sections such as "A", "B", "C", etc.

Once they are grouped together, **turn those phrases into sentences.** Take your notes, data, and information and write it out into complete thoughts. Those sentences form your paragraphs.

Then **move the paragraphs around** to flow in a logical order. The order can be chronological or any order the reader would expect. I typically begin with the most important paragraphs and end with the least important.

Lastly, add **transitions between each paragraph.** That is my formula for brainstorming and writing. If you're stuck, refer to my list of transition words in the appendix.

The 3 Brainstorming Methods

Next, I'm going to teach you 3 methods to brainstorm your message before you actually write:

- Free Writing
- Mind Mapping
- Outlining

Let's continue on and learn each of these techniques right now.

Free Write

The first brainstorming technique is free writing.

On a piece of paper, write out everything you can think of regarding your topic. It is a "brain dump". By unlocking the data that's been "filed away" in your mind, you access your creative side.

When writing with a pen, your creative juices will start to flow as you tap into the right creative side of your brain. Don't edit or censor as you write.

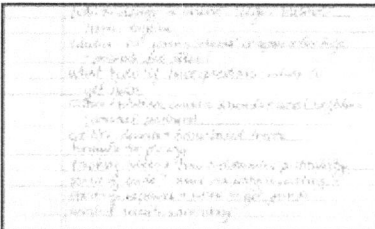

Free writing is a great way to get started in advance of sitting down to write. You tap into existing information hidden away in your brain. It helps you get a huge head start on your message.

Now that you've written out your thoughts, how do you convert that messy text to an organized outline? That's the next step: grouping and organizing.

In my free writing, I jot down everything that comes to mind, whether it's messy or not. You can see my sample paper has scribbles, cross-outs, and arrows.

Then, I use my color highlighters to highlight items that are similar. And I put numbers or letters in front of each "group" of similar items. This is the beginning of an effective outline, which forms the basis for your document.

Mind Map

The second technique is called mind mapping.
Mind mapping is similar to free writing — it is
brainstorming but using a spatial concept.

To create a mind map,
start with your topic in the
middle of the paper.
Circle it. As you can see in
my example, our topic is
"Start a Kid Biz".

From the circled topic,
draw some lines projecting out of that circle. Each
of those legs should have a bubble attached to it.
They are your sub-topics.

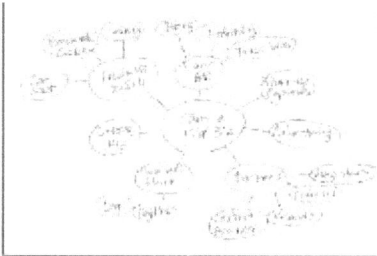

In my example, "Start a
Kid Biz", you can see
that the sub-topics
include: Products to
Sell, Earn Money, and
Start-Up Expenses.
These items will turn
into the chapters.

Each of those sub-topics could have more lines
coming out from them. Jutting out from those will
be more messages, and those are your actual notes.
These notes will be turned into sentences and then
developed into paragraphs for each chapter.

The great thing about mind mapping is that it allows your brain to think spatially, in a creative manner, instead of logically. It helps you generate new ideas. Once you have your entire mind map done, now you can take that and convert those phrases into sentences, paragraphs, and chapters.

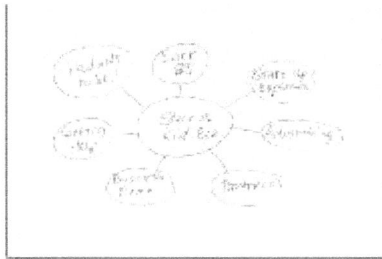

MindMapper Software

One more cool tool that I love is called **MindMapper software**. It is a wonderful software because it allows you to start with your topic, brainstorm sub-topics, and list points under each sub-topic in a spatial format. It's exactly like when you wrote out your mind map in the previous example.

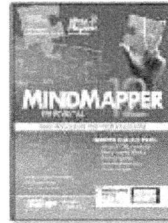

This magic software automatically turns your mind map into a topical outline with the click of a button.

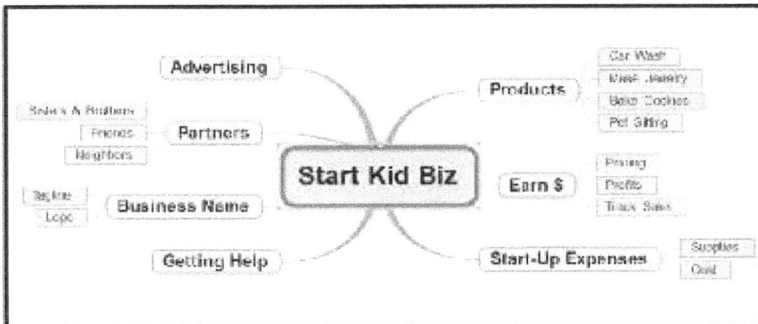

In this illustration, you can see the same topic, "Start a Kid Biz", brainstormed into the MindMapper software. The topic is a bright blue box in the middle of the page. The sub-topics are in yellow boxes connected to the topic. And the notes are gray boxes connected to the corresponding sub-topics. Now let's find out how to turn this creative, spatial format into a logical outline!

Here you can see the how MindMapper12 turned the mindmap into an outline, which was then exported into Word® as a topical outline.

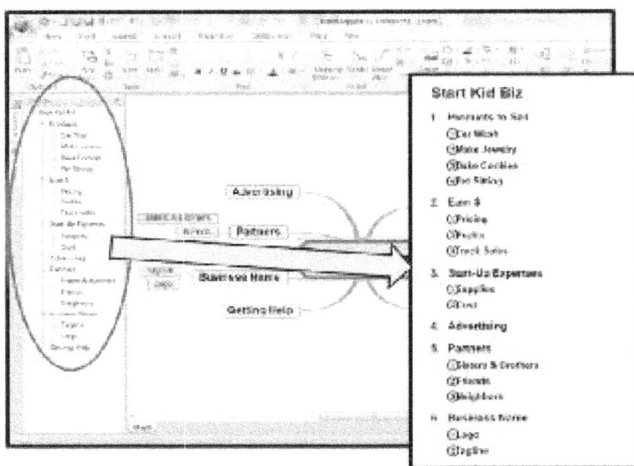

The reason I love this method so much is because you start with the spatial format and tap into the creative side of your brain. Then you use the computer to automatically turn it into the logical format that you need to begin writing.

How would you like a demo of MindMapper software in action? I made a fun and quick demo video to show you exactly how it works. You'll find it on our Queen Bee Publisher's youtube page. Check it out!

Topical Outline

My third technique is to **use an outline format.** If you are an analytical person and your brain thinks in a methodical manner, an outline is the best way for you to start. An outline is a skeleton, or backbone, of your project.

A **topical outline** starts with your main topic. Under the topic, write each sub-topic and leave 4 or 5 blank lines. Under each of the sub-topics, fill in the blank lines with phrases, bullet points, or numbers. They don't need to be complete sentences, just thoughts or ideas.

The sub-topics do not have to be in any particular order. Remember you can move around the sub-topics once your document is typed out. The important thing is to get all of your thoughts from your head onto paper.

In conclusion, now you know how to brainstorm using my favorite methods. Put these 3 super power tools in your toolbox!

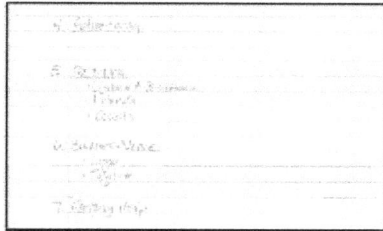

Activities

Now that you have learned 3 super power tools to break through writer's block, it's your turn to practice them now. Get out 3 sheets of paper and pen to complete the activities below:

1. Free write about your document topic for 10 minutes. Just write down any and all thoughts that come to mind. Don't edit as you write it out.

2. Draw a mind map with your topic in the middle. Draw bubbles around the center bubble, then complete each bubble with your sub-topics. Then draw more bubbles for your content ideas.

3. Organize an outline with your topic. Write the main topic at the top, and 5 sub-topics underneath, with 4 lines between each. Then fill in the sub-topics with content.

Using these 3 brainstorming and data-organizing techniques can help skyrocket you to success.

5. Gain Momentum

Now you know how to prepare yourself for writing. You learned specific techniques for overcoming writer's block and you have power tools available to you. Let's continue on and build momentum.

Momentum is the power of motion continuing on. For example to get a tire to start rolling, you have to give it a push. But once it started, it continues to roll on its own, fueled by its own momentum. The same thing happens to you when you begin writing. The more you write, the more momentum you will have to continue going forward. We will discuss a few ways to continue your momentum and complete your book, report, or writing project.

Become a Better Writer

Here are 4 strategies to become a better writer. They are simple to start doing right now.

Read Every Day

The first tip is to **read more**. No matter what you read, it will help you become a better writer. Why is that? First of all, you see words and context, and you will understand the correct meaning of new words. You will also learn to differentiate between commonly confused words like "they're", "their" and "there" when you see them in the proper context.

Begin a habit of reading every day. You can select from a novel, an autobiography, a science fiction story, a romance novel, a "how to" book, business research, student assignments, personal development, or the Bible. Put aside time in your schedule every morning or evening to read 30 minutes every day. You'll be surprised at how much your writing improves when you read more.

It's never too late to become a good reader. One day, I visited my grandpa when he was about 75 years old. He had a book on the table and I was amazed because I've never seen him read anything before. When he grew up, education was not valued like it is today. He worked on a family ranch and only went to school through 5th grade. After a military career, he paved roads with his loader. His hobby? Welding. He never needed to read. So I was shocked to find a Zane Grey western novel on his dining room table and I asked, "Grandpa, whose book is this?" He said, "It's mine." Surprised, I exclaimed, "You're reading it?" He said, "Yes! I've read 3 Zane Grey novels so far." He was truly enjoying this late-life skill. The life lesson I learned is that it's **never too late** to begin reading.

If you don't like reading, I suggest starting with audio books. You can listen as you drive in your car. Next, try reading a printed book as you listen to its audio book. If you prefer to read digital books on your computer, phone or tablet, that's great too. Keep reading every day. Make it a daily habit.

Practice Writing

Then second way to become a better writer is to **write more**. When you take action, your hand and your mind practice writing and they are prepared for more action. Get in the habit of writing because it eliminates procrastination. And that helps you become a better writer.

Ask for Feedback

In addition to guidebooks, **get feedback from others**. Feedback means constructive criticism, critiques, or edits to our writing. It's very difficult to get critiqued on our writing, isn't it? We put our heart and soul into our stories. We pour ourselves into our document and when someone critiques our writing, it can hurt. However painful it may be, it's important to get that necessary feedback.

When you get feedback, it doesn't mean the feedback has to be from a professional editor, the grammar police, or someone with a degree in English. Feedback can come from anyone who's willing to take a few moments and look over your document, and give you some kind, constructive criticism or friendly feedback.

As our writing gets edited and proofread, we learn professional techniques and develop skills. Without feedback, our writing will be stifled and suffer.

Use Your Resources

And lastly, use your resources. Consult reference books. Find information through sources such as the lexis-nexis database, or leatherby libraries (a subsidiary of Chapman University). Go to professional trade journals for your industry.

So those are the 4 ways to become a better writer: read more, write more, get feedback, and use your resources. Make those each a daily habit for you.

Effective Writing

Dr. Jim Howland, my favorite tech writing professor at Cal Poly, had a favorite saying. He taught us that "Effective writing means saying everything that needs to be said, and nothing that doesn't." What does this mean?

If you're a person who's long-winded and your prose includes a lot of narrative, go back and edit out the extra wording. Cut down your text to the basics that your readers need to hear. Eliminate babble and clichés to give your readers a clear path to your message.

On the other hand, if you're a bottom-line person who's known to be blunt, expand your content to build bridges for your readers. Help them see the big picture by including background information, adding transitions, and explaining how the information relates to your reader.

As you write, keep that definition in mind. "Effective writing means saying everything that needs to be said, and nothing that doesn't." Constantly test your content to make sure it meets these guidelines by asking yourself, "Did I say everything important that my reader needs to know? Did I eliminate the fluff that may distract my reader?"

Burger Writing Method

Who's hungry? Maybe you've worked up an appetite reading this book, and you're ready for a burger. If so, you're in the right place. This illustration will help you remember all the content pieces for your document.

Even if you're hungry, you probably wouldn't eat a plain hamburger patty. It's greasy and boring and looks "blah". There's nothing attractive about it. But when we give our readers only the core "meat" of our message, it's like handing them a plain meat patty. It is not appetizing.

Our readers want more than just the "meat". Add melted cheese, veggies, condiments, top and bottom buns, and the burger looks delicious. It becomes an entire meal. That's what your readers are craving — the entire appetizing experience.

In your document, the opening (introduction) is like a top bun. It draws in your reader and helps to "contain" the message. When you write your overview (summary), it's like adding colorful, crunchy veggies and melty cheese. Then you bite into the meat (main points), upon which to expound and discuss. It's hearty, delicious, and yet digestible. Your summary obviously summarizes your document. It is comparable to those all-important tasty condiments that add spice and seasoning. Lastly, your conclusion (call to action or happy ending) is like the bottom bun. The buns contain your message by holding everything together in a nice, neat package.

A burger is easy for your reader to grasp and understand your message. From the burger, you learned that your document must have 5 main parts. It's similar to the "essay" format in grade school, but a lot more fun. When you get stuck, just think about burger writing. Keep that visual in mind and you'll break through writer's block to a beautifully finished document.

Openings & Closings

Now that you know the importance of attention-getting openings and powerful closings, I'll show you some ideas to help you elevate your writing.

Your opening determines whether someone will read your document and stay engaged. Never start with narrative — it'll bore your readers and they won't stay tuned. A critical key to success is to start with a strong, powerful opening.

Interesting **openings** may begin with:

- A short, heart-warming story
- An example related to your topic
- A demonstration of how someone's life has improved by applying your message
- A quote from a famous person
- Identifying with the reader's problems, concerns, challenges, or obstacles
- An expert's assessment of the topic

At the end of your document, add a **closing** that motivates your reader to action. If your book is a "how-to guide", a call to action gets your reader going. For a novel or fiction story, insert a warm, happy ending.

A great closing leaves your reader with an upbeat feeling. Keep the following in mind about closings:

- A closing makes the reader feel good about themselves, the message, and you.
- Closings should motivate, encourage, and inspire your readers.
- If you need your reader to DO something, include a call to action with a date, time, and place.

To get more great ideas for openings and closings, I recommend the reference book, "Effective Business Writing", specifically pages 72 and 73. You'll find practical ideas, along with examples, of how to open and close your document. I love this little book and recommend it to my writing students. Every page is packed with powerful tips. You can find it online at www.OurBookStore.com .

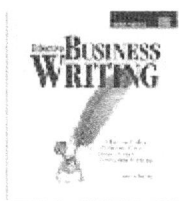

Activities

Here are 3 simple activities you can incorporate into your daily routine to sharpen your writing skills.

1. Write down the titles of 2 books you have on hand, which you will begin reading today. Take a moment and put "reading" into your schedule for 30 minutes per day, either morning, evening, or both.

2. Think about the BURGER writing method. How can you incorporate the 5 levels (openings, introduction, main points, conclusion, and closing) into each document you write?

3. Identify 3 reference books that can help you refine your writing skills. Include at least 1 style guide. Write down the titles of these reference guides. If you don't already have them on hand, order them now.

By implementing these good everyday practices, you will improve your writing and become a better communicator.

6. Keep Going Strong

Now you have the power of momentum on your side. In this section, we're going to continue building upon your knowledge base by explaining resources you can print out and use when writing.

Also, you'll get a sneak peak of more great writing courses that you might be interested in and book-writing coaching to keep you progressing forward. We're here to support and guide you in all of your writing needs. So let's keep on going strong!

Bonus Resources

Your gift today is the 3 bonus "cheat sheets" at the end of this book. The first list is Grammar Guide, followed by Vibrant Verbs and then Transition Terms. These are my extremely valuable resources that took me years to compile. I'm giving them to you here today free as a book bonus.

Let's find out more about each valuable bonus list.

Grammar Guide

As you edit your document, you'll notice the importance of word usage. Are your words spelled correctly? Did you use the correct words? Can you substitute a better term, such as a synonym? Did you eliminate passive sentences?

Spelling Errors

When editing your document, 2 important types of words to check are:

- Misspelled words
- Misused words

Misspelled words are words you spelled wrong. Your spell checker will probably catch these words. That's the good news.

The bad news is that **misused words** are difficult to find and correct because your spell checker does not catch them. They are words commonly confused with other words because they're spelled similarly, sound similarly, or have similar meanings. For example: "there", "they're" and "their" are spelled 3 different ways. These similar-sounding words are often misused and confused.

Word confusion is common because the American English language is a mish-mash of other languages that has evolved over the years. Grammar and spelling rules seem to have exceptions for every rule! Word spellings can be weird and wacky, defying logic or reasoning. So if you're a bit spelling-challenged, don't worry. Many people make these same mistakes. Many word spellings seem to have no "rhyme or reason".

The challenge is: how to use the correct words in each sentence? My smart solution is to **keep a cheat sheet by your desk.** Then, you don't have to look up these words every time, especially if they're words you misspell frequently. Just refer to your cheat sheet of correct words. After a while, you'll start to memorize them.

Copy my "Grammar Guide" which includes both commonly confused words and many misspelled words. How is that for convenience! Simply print the handout, insert in a clear plastic sheet protector, and keep it by your desk for easy reference. Feel free to add your own challenging words to this list. Don't stumble and fumble for the right word. Reference this sheet when you're stuck.

Synonyms

As you read your text, you'll recognize words you used repeatedly throughout your writing project. Change it up and vary the format by substituting other words with the same meaning, known as synonyms. In school we used to open up a big Thesaurus and look up the word. Today, you can find a handy thesaurus online at www.Dictionary.com .

An even simpler way to insert synonyms is to right-click on the word and a context menu pops up in Microsoft® Word®. Hover over "Synonyms" and select a new word. How easy is that! It's an awesome tech tool built into Word®. Be aware that it does not work every time, because some words have multiple meanings. But with most words, it can certainly save you time and effort while elevating your prose!

Grammar Check

Did you know that you can set up a **customized grammar check** in Word®? It will check for common grammatical errors and give you suggestions to improve your writing style. Leverage built-in tools. Work smarter, not harder.

Click File > Options > Proofing. Under the field Writing Style > Grammar & Style > Settings, click and select your preferred styles. Once it's set up, you will see words or phrases with the blue zig-zag underline. Right-click on them, then click "Grammar" to see the explanation and suggestions.

For example, I set up my grammar check to highlight passive sentences and verb phrases. Checking those items livens up writing livelier and more action oriented.

Vibrant Action Verbs

The first bonus handout is **action verbs**. I challenge you to eliminate blah, boring, do-nothing verbs from your writing. Instead, substitute alive action verbs. Action verbs make your story come to life. You give the readers specific direction. You motivate them to get up and DO something.

I've included **148 action verbs** here that will help take your documents from boring and blah to exciting, interesting, and engaging. When giving your reader tasks or a procedural list, start each item with an action verb. Instead of the generic verb in "Let's **do** it," can you see how much more meaningful it is to say, "Let's **organize** this now" or "Let's **solve** it" or "Let's **compile** it." The action verb makes a huge difference!

Action verbs are not only interesting, they're more specific because they convey a more exact meaning. You're not limited to these 148 words, of course. You can collect more and add to your list, but this is a great way to get you started.

When writer's block strikes and you just can't construct the next sentence, pull out your action verbs. Look through the list, pick a few, and get going. Come on, what are you waiting for?

Transition Phrases & Terms

After you've written your content and moved your paragraphs in the correct order, ensure you have a logical flow between paragraphs and thoughts. And that's where these transition words come in handy. Using the right transitions can make a difference between an amateur document and a professional sounding document.

Now, let's look at the awesome bonus list called **Transition Terms**. You'll see words, phrases, and terms that smooth your flow. They give direction to your paragraphs, link your thoughts together, and help your reader move from one thought to the next. Transitions create a cohesive document.

Here is my **best collection**! During my writing career, I collected these wonderful transition words and organized them by type. For the first time, I'm pulling back the curtain and revealing all 197 terms. **Nearly 200 great phrases** to help you write and edit.

And those are your 3 dynamic bonus items from Queen Bee Publisher, Inc.

Hungry for More Courses?

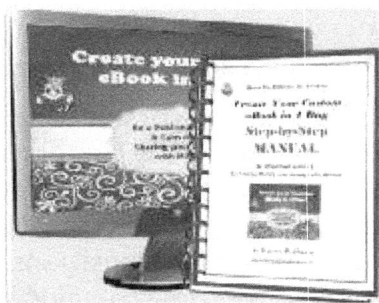

Would you like to learn more about writing? Have you dreamed about authoring an eBook? Are you ready to tackle that long overdue novel or how-to book? What about writing your life story — leaving a legacy and a record of your memoirs for your heirs?

What about friends and family who can benefit from your knowledge? Putting your thoughts and ideas into a book is a great way to prove your credibility and expertise in a topic and leave a lasting legacy.

If you're interested in continuing along this learning path in your writing career, we offer a course called "Create Your Custom eBook in 1 Day". In this course, we show you how to start with an idea or a topic and develop that into an eBook. We walk you through every step of creating chapters, headings, and organizing it into a logical flow. We then show you how to polish your book by editing and proofreading with a partner, how to format the text using Microsoft Word tools, and publish your book on to Kindle or other sources such as Lulu.

Marketing is very important once you've finished your eBook. In this course, we touch on the topics of promoting your ebook. If you liked this book "Breaking Through Writer's Block", then you will love our course "Create Your Custom eBook". It includes 7 additional bonus forms and live video demos of various techniques to write quicker, faster, and easier. Take the next step. Celebrate your success by moving up to the next level!

Book Coaching

Attention authors! Would you like additional assistance getting your book published? We're here to assist you with our book coaching programs. Select from Bronze, Silver, Gold, or our ultimate Platinum programs.

Bronze Program

Our "Bronze Book Coaching Program" is for aspiring authors who are ready to take the self-study course and complete the book on their own. It includes the complete kit: access to our online course, step-by-step manual, bonus forms, and links to computer demos. It also includes the following: ISBN code, QR code, formatted book template, and one private coaching session to help you initially select your book topic.

Silver Program

Our "Silver Book Coaching Program" is for aspiring authors who want to complete a book on their own, but need the guidance and accountability of a coach to stay focused and get it completed quickly. We coach you privately from start to finish with weekly coaching sessions as you create your own book in 60 days. It also includes everything in the Bronze program: online course, step-by-step manual, bonus forms, computer demos, ISBN code, QR code, book template, and 10 copies of your printed book!

Gold Program

Our "Gold Book Coaching Program", is for aspiring authors who don't want to write the book themselves. They are willing to compile and send us their content, and smart enough to delegate the project completion to us. You supply the content we request, and with our private coaching sessions we magically create a book for you in 60 days. It also includes everything in the Silver program: access to our online course, step-by-step manual, bonus forms, computer demos, ISBN code, QR code, book template, and 10 copies of your printed book!

Platinum Program

Or, if you want to completely delegate the entire project, we'll do it all! You don't have to write, edit, or type anything. Select the "Platinum / Ultimate Book Author Program" and our writing team will interview you, gather the content, and create your custom book for you. This top tier program includes ISBN code, publishing services, and 10 copies of your printed book ready for you to autograph and share with friends.

Consider joining one of our book coaching programs today. We can help you from start to finish: beginning with your idea or concept, deciding on a topic, getting it written, edited, polished, and most importantly, seeing your book published. Imagine your joy when you hold the first copy of your printed book in your hand.

Activities

Here are a few more fun activities to keep you going strong in your career as a business professional:

1. Copy the "Action Verbs" bonus list. Make a commitment to stop using the 4 blah verbs (have, be, got, do). Circle 10 action verbs that you like. Now, substitute these action verbs instead of blah verbs.

2. Copy the "Grammar Guide" bonus list. To the list, add at least 3 words that you often misspell. Put the handout into a clear plastic sheet protector and put it by your desk for quick reference.

3. Copy the "Transition Words" bonus list. Circle 5 terms that you would like to incorporate into your paragraphs. Start using them today!

Writing doesn't have to be boring. The process can be fascinating and even enjoyable. Stimulate your mind by writing more each day.

7. Conclusion

Let's recap what we've learned, take action steps, and keep moving forward. You've gained momentum so keep going and leverage it for your success.

Action Steps

The writing process is simple and becomes a habit after practice. Jot down your **action steps** for the topic you're writing about:

1. Gather the content
2. Collect your writing tools
3. Brainstorm your message
4. Group your sub-topics together
5. Write your material
6. Organize your document
7. Edit and proofread
8. Finalize your project!

Take your steps to success **NOW**. Every minute you wait, your dream is deferred. After putting it off for a while, your dream begins to diminish. Keep your dream alive by starting right now while it's fresh in your mind and you are excited. I know you can do it! And you will, because only YOU can communicate your unique message to the world. Your audience is ready and eager to benefit from **your message**.

Summary

To recap and review all of the many things we've learned in this course.

1. Introduction – why we get writer's block and the benefits of breaking through.

2. "Get Started Right" showed you how to set a solid foundation for success. In this section, you learned how to create good everyday writing habits. I showed you how to select a topic, speak authentically, gather your content, and compile writing tools.

3. "Solutions for Every Situation" was the heart of our course. We identified 12 of the most common causes of writer's block, and explored 38 techniques to combat them and propel you to victory.

4. In "Super Power Tools" we learned 3 tried-and-true strategies to brainstorm ideas onto paper: free writing, mind mapping, and creating a topical outline.

5. "Gain Momentum". In this section, we discussed how to become a better writer, and the value of reading every day. Also I showed you my secret formula called "BURGER" writing.

6. The "Keep Going Strong" section explained the 3 free bonus handouts you received with this course. I revealed additional courses and coaching programs available for your professional and personal development.

7. My 3 "Bonus Forms" are available for you in the appendix here at the end of the book.

Packed with tons of content, this book offers you the best of all worlds: accessible techniques, expert tips, and tools you can put to use immediately.

Contact Me

Please write me — I would love to hear your success stories. Do you have questions, concerns, or friendly feedback? If so, feel free to reach out. Here's my contact information. You can reach me via email at info@queenbeepublisher.com and on our website, www.queenbeepublisher.com. Our youtube video demos are also posted.

Thank You

Thank you very much for reading our book. We enjoyed your company here with us today and hope you will join us for our other books, online courses, and audio training.

Bonus Resources

Following are my bonus forms for you to use at your desk when writing:

- Grammar Guide
- Transition Terms
- Vibrant Verbs

Chapter 6, "Keep Going Strong", gives instructions on how to use each of the 3 forms.

Grammar Guide

Commonly Confused Words

- accept / except
- advice / advise
- affect / effect
- alright / all right
- assure / insure / ensure
- by / bye / buy
- capital / Capitol
- compliment / complement
- conscious / conscience / conscientious
- council / counsel
- farther / further
- fewer / less
- forth / fourth / forty
- forward / foreword
- good / well
- imply / infer
- it's / its
- loose / lose
- maybe / may be
- moral / morale
- personal / personnel
- perspective / prospective
- precede / proceed
- principal / principle
- preceding / proceeding
- realty / reality
- resume / résumé
- sale / sell
- stationary / stationery
- then / than
- they're / their / there
- through / thorough
- to / too / two
- very / vary
- way / weigh
- weather / whether
- which / that
- who / whom
- whose / who's
- you're / your
- write / right

Many Misspelled Business Words

- accommodate
- acknowledgment
- appendix / appendices (plural)
- argument
- beautiful
- bureaucratic
- calendar
- column
- congratulations
- consensus
- copyright
- deductible
- dilemma
- eighth
- embarrass
- entrepreneur
- excited
- existence
- experience
- harass
- height
- hors d'oeuvres
- indispensable
- judgment
- knowledgeable
- lien
- lieu (in lieu of)
- liaison
- license
- miscellaneous
- occasion
- occurrence
- persevere
- privilege
- proceed
- procedures
- queue
- receipt
- receive
- relevant
- rescind
- ridiculous
- schedule
- separate
- supersede
- tally
- vice versa

Words NOT to Use

Instead of:	Use:
alot	a lot
costed	cost
hopefully	I hope
invaluable	valuable
irregardless	regardless
literally	really
OK	okay
oral	verbal
preventative	preventive

Vibrant Verbs

Accept	Conduct	Expand
Achieve	Confirm	Explain
Advise	Connect	File
Administer	Conserve	Fill out
Aid	Contact	Find
Analyze	Convey	Finish
Approve	Coordinate	Follow up
Ask	Correct	Forward
Assign	Create	Gain
Assist	Decide	Gather
Attach	Delete	Generate
Attain	Deliver	Give
Authorize	Describe	Guide
Begin	Design	Help
Benefit	Detach	Hold
Build	Determine	Identify
Buy	Develop	Implement
Calculate	Discuss	Improve
Capture	Distribute	Increase
Charge	Email	Inspect
Check	Encourage	Install
Claim	Enforce	Interview
Close	Enter	Instruct
Compile	Ensure	Invite
Complete	Establish	Issue
Concentrate	Evaluate	Keep
Conclude	Examine	Lead

Break Through Writer's Block

List	Purchase	Sign
Mail	Push	Solve
Maintain	Raise	Sort
Manage	Read	Start
Measure	Receive	Submit
Merge	Recommend	Survey
Negotiate	Record	Teach
Notify	Reduce	Test
Obtain	Release	Thank
Open	Remove	Tighten
Operate	Repeat	Total
Order	Report	Train
Organize	Research	Transfer
Participate	Resolve	Turn
Pay	Request	Use
Place	Review	Validate
Plan	Rotate	Value
Prepare	Schedule	Verify
Print	Select	View
Produce	Sell	Wait
Protect	Send	Withdraw
Prove	Separate	Write
Provide	Serve	
Pull	Show	

Transition Terms

Add	Also	In addition
	And	With that
	Besides	
Anticipation	As a matter of fact	Of course
	For that matter	Surely
	It follows that	To be expected
	Naturally	
Comparison	Alternately	Less than
	Compared to	More than
	In comparison	On the other hand
Concessions	Certainly	Of course
	Doubtless	To be certain
	Granted that	To be sure
	No doubt that	
Consequence	As a result	So
	Consequently	Therefore
	Due to	Unfortunately
Continuing	Besides	Furthermore
	Further	In addition
Contradiction	Although	Even so
	And yet	Nevertheless
	Despite	Nonetheless
Emphasis	Again	Indeed
	Especially	Most importantly
	In any case	
End	Again	Lastly
	Finally	Since
	In conclusion	To summarize
	In short	
Extra	Additionally	Indeed
	Furthermore	Moreover
	In fact	

Future	The next time	Looking forward
	In the future	
Illustrate	A sample is	Likewise
	For example	Similarly
	For instance	To illustrate
	In the same way	
Location	Above	Between
	Approximately	Beyond
	Below	Next to
	Beside	
Order	Afterwards	Subsequently
	Following this	Thereafter
	Previously	While
Paraphrase	In other words	What that means is
	Just like	To put it another way
	Or	
Qualify	Always	Particularly
	Frequently	Specifically
	Generally	Typically
	Occasionally	Usually
	Often	
Reasons	Another reason	For
	Because	Since
	Due to	Which
Reflection	Earlier	In the past
	Looking Back	Previously
Restrictions	If provided	Provided that
	In case	Unless
	Lest	When
	Only	
Result	Accordingly	On the whole
	As a consequence	Thus
	For this reason	Therefore
	Hence	

Reverse	Although	Still
	But	Though
	However	Whereas
	In Contrast	Yet
Sequence	First	After
	Second	Next
	Third	Then
	Fourth	Last
Similarity	As	Once more
	Like	Similarly
	Likewise	In the same manner
Summary	All in all	In summary
	Altogether	Once again
	In brief	Therefore
	In conclusion	This means
Time	At last	In the future
	Before	Meanwhile
	Beforehand	Presently
	Briefly	Simultaneously
	By that time	
Transition	From then on	Now that
	In the meantime	
Urgency	At the moment	Presently
	Currently	Shortly
	Immediately	Soon
	Now	Soon after

Index

accept less than perfect 35

acknowledge your experience level.................45

action steps...95

Activities 30, 64, 76, 84, 94

analysis paralysis..37

ask for help 49

ask mentor for help 43

audience of avatars 62

authentic voice...................................... 12, 17

begin while you're excited 57

better writer 77

book coaching 91

brainstorm 68

burger writing 81

causes 31

choose a grateful attitude...........................51

closings 82

copy a successful person............................46

data overload...42

delegate to assistant 43

distractions 40

everyday habits 7

examples 18

faith beats fear 51

feeling stuck...54

few resources 48

free write 70

gather content 15

get comfortable with messy.........................34

get cooperation 41

get rid of info 42

get started now 52
grammar guide 85
Grammar Guide BONUS 100
healthy routine 50
inspiration 8, 9
job overload 42
just do it 37
just say no 51
message 7, 11, 13, 17, 23, 25, 27, 28, 29, 34, 36, 38,
   62, 68, 70, 81
micro break 60
milestones 3
mind map 72
motivational messages 55
move the deadline 52
narrate the boring 38
NON-Writing 27
not confident 45
openings 82
outline 75
overwhelmed 42
partner up with friend 43
perfectionist 34
picture your goals 62
procrastination 56
quick deadline 52
re-arrange your priorities 53
relocate to a quiet place 40
research 16
reverse self-sabotage 56
self-discipline 41
soft background music 59
solutions 31
stagnant environment 58
start with the easy part first 54
stay one step ahead 46

stories 18

stress 50

stretch break 61

super power tools....................................67

tackle the tiny..57

take a break 60

timer – break - timer 54

tool prep 48

topic pondering 49

transition terms.......................................89

Transition Terms BONUS 105

try something new & zany........................59

unfocused 60

vary your routine 58

vibrant verbs 88

Vibrant Verbs BONUS 102

visualize the connection 38

voice recognition software 24

voice recorder........................9, 23, 30, 36, 37

walking break 61

what if..9

write from your heart................................35

writer's block.....................1, 2, 31, 46, 65, 77

writing tools 20

More Books and Courses

from *Queen Bee Publisher, Inc.*

	Buy Your First Home: A Basic Step-by-Step Guide for First Time Home Buyers • Paperback • eBook • Audio book • Online course • Hardback
	Learn the Lingo of Houses: Reference of Real Estate Terms for Today's Industry Professionals • Paperback • eBook
	2016 Goal Achiever: Daily Planner for Winning Real Estate Professionals • Full size spiral bound • Pocket size spiral bound • Desk Binder Kit with highlighters

	Create Your Custom eBook in 1 Day: Share Your Message, Earn Money, & Reach Millions • Online course • eGuide
	Break Through Writer's Block: Invigorate Your Mind, Generate New Ideas, & Voice Your Authentic Message Powerfully • Paperback • eBook • Online course
	Lease a Commercial Business Building: Small Business Owners and Entrepreneurs — Negotiate Your Best Deal • Online course
	Super Sales Strategies: Customer Service Reference for Retailers • eBook • Online course
	Kids, Open Your Art Shop Today: Create & Sell Your Handmade Crafts • eBook • Online course

www.ingramcontent.com/pod-product-compliance
Lightning Source LLC
Chambersburg PA
CBHW021341090426
42742CB00008B/697